EIGHTEENTH-CENTURY ITALIAN PORCELAIN

CLARE LE CORBEILLER

ASSOCIATE CURATOR
DEPARTMENT OF EUROPEAN SCULPTURE
AND DECORATIVE ARTS

THE METROPOLITAN MUSEUM OF ART

This publication has been made possible by a generous grant from The Joseph H. and Florence A. Roblee Foundation.

Library of Congress Cataloging in Publication Data

Le Corbeiller, Clare.
Eighteenth-century Italian porcelain.

Bibliography: p.
1. Porcelain, Italian. 2. Porcelain—18th century—Italy. I. Title.
NK4503.L4 1985 738'.0945 85-5063
ISBN 0-87099-421-2 (pbk.)

Published by The Metropolitan Museum of Art
Bradford D. Kelleher, Publisher
John P. O'Neill, Editor in Chief
Polly Cone, Project supervisor
Kuan Chang, Designer

Photography by the Photograph Studio, The Metropolitan Museum of Art

Typeset by U. S. Lithograph Inc., New York
Printed and bound by Meridian Printing, East Greenwich, Rhode Island

On the cover: 18. *Dancing Couple.* Capodimonte, 1750–55

ISBN POD edition: 978-0-300-20080-5
Printer/binder POD edition: Acme Bookbinding, Charlestown, MA

FOREWORD

Included in the Museum's comprehensive collections are many smaller ones that illustrate facets of the intriguing history of styles and techniques. It is with a view to making these sometimes subtle qualities more widely known that we here inaugurate a new publishing venture—a series of informative, well-illustrated, and accessible guides.

This summary handbook of eighteenth-century Italian porcelain is the first of the new booklets designed to focus on aspects of the Museum's larger collections. I especially thank Clare Le Corbeiller, Associate Curator in the Department of European Sculpture and Decorative Arts, who undertook the launching of the series with such admirable results. In addition, I express my deep thanks to The Joseph H. and Florence A. Roblee Foundation for conceiving and generously supporting a program that fulfills so essential a part of the Museum's educational role.

Philippe de Montebello, Director
The Metropolitan Museum of Art

The earliest European porcelain was made in Florence under the patronage of Francesco I de' Medici, grand duke of Tuscany. It was inspired by the blue and white hard-paste porcelains being imported from China, but, unlike them, was composed of different elements. Kaolin, the clay that is essential to hard paste, was not discovered in Europe until the eighteenth century. Substitute formulas, using white clays mixed with varying combinations of lime and other ingredients, such as steatite or alabaster, produced so-called soft-paste bodies. As the first of these, Medici porcelain was of exceptional importance both as an accomplishment and for the amalgamation of oriental, Near Eastern, and High Renaissance styles in its forms and decoration. It was also a unique, isolated phenomenon: the enterprise came to an end with Francesco's death in 1587, and, although there is evidence of scattered production up to the 1630s, systematic porcelain manufacture in Italy only began in the following century.

The eighteenth-century Italian factories were highly regional in character. Whereas Meissen generated a dozen factories in Germany that took their cue from its repertoire, and Sèvres in France succeeded in imposing broad stylistic authority, the Italian factories had little influence on each other.

This is not to say they were unaware of each other, or of developments in northern Europe. Competition encouraged a constant movement of arcanists, modelers, and decorators who carried techniques and styles from one country and factory to another; and subtler influences may be traced in, for example, the training in one region of an artist whose career was spent in another.

But Italy's political history argued against stylistic unity: in the mid-eighteenth century Venice was still the center of an independent republic, Tuscany owed allegiance to Austria, and Naples belonged to the Bourbons. However temporary these political arrangements, they invited a certain cultural isolation and afforded their own implications in terms of patronage and artistic contacts and influence.

VENICE AND THE NORTHERN FACTORIES

The first of the eighteenth-century factories was founded in Venice in 1720 at the instigation of Francesco Vezzi (1651–1740), who had been trained—and briefly practiced—as a goldsmith but turned his attention to financial and mercantile affairs. How he came to be interested in porcelain is not known, but in 1719 he was in Vienna, where Claude Du Paquier (d. 1751) had established his own manufactory the preceding year; and it was from Vienna that Vezzi provided the financial backing and authorization for his son, Giovanni, to proceed with a similar undertaking in Venice. It was also in Vienna that Vezzi must have met Christoph Conrad Hunger (active ca. 1717–ca. 1748), who at that time was working for Du Paquier. Sometime in 1720 Hunger fled to Venice, and in 1721 he is recorded as one of the partners in the Vezzi enterprise.

Throughout the eighteenth century, almost without exception, porcelain factories were started with the help of workmen whose real or supposed expertise was strongly in demand, and who were thus encouraged to move from place to place. Hunger had been at Dresden and, although not then an employee of Meissen, appears to have been able to bring—first to Vienna, then to Venice—two crucial pieces of assistance: access to the same deposits of kaolin (the high-firing white clay essential to hard-paste porcelain) as used at Meissen and Vienna, and some experience with the technology of colors.

Vezzi's factory was in operation for only seven years, and it has been estimated that fewer than two hundred pieces have survived. Most of these are teapots and related small tablewares. Because it was only the third hard-paste factory in Europe —following Meissen (1710) and Vienna—there was still a limited repertoire of forms for the material, and Vezzi, out of necessity and as a natural consequence of his background, often drew on metalwork forms for his models. The most frequently encountered object is the teapot, which exists in a number of original, experimental models. The Museum's example (1) is characteristic of Vezzi work in its faceted form, its echoes of silversmithing, its low-relief decoration, and its sparing use of strong color, which seems suspended in the white space of the field. Other models, more sharply polygonal, are dramatized by angular handles, tapered bodies, and crisply molded ornament.

Also common are slender handleless beakers, sometimes molded with bands of upright leaves in the manner of—and almost indistinguishable from—Meissen and Vienna, or with prunus branches or garlands. The decoration of Vezzi porcelains was strongly influenced by the fashion for oriental styles. The lively figures on the Museum's teapot are derived (and possibly molded) from similar ones on Chinese blanc de chine cups being exported to Europe at the time. Other decorations in the oriental style include tropical-looking landscapes, long-necked imaginary birds that swoop somewhat awkwardly through space, and highly stylized flowers on thin, undulating stems, reminiscent of those on Indian chintzes of the early eighteenth

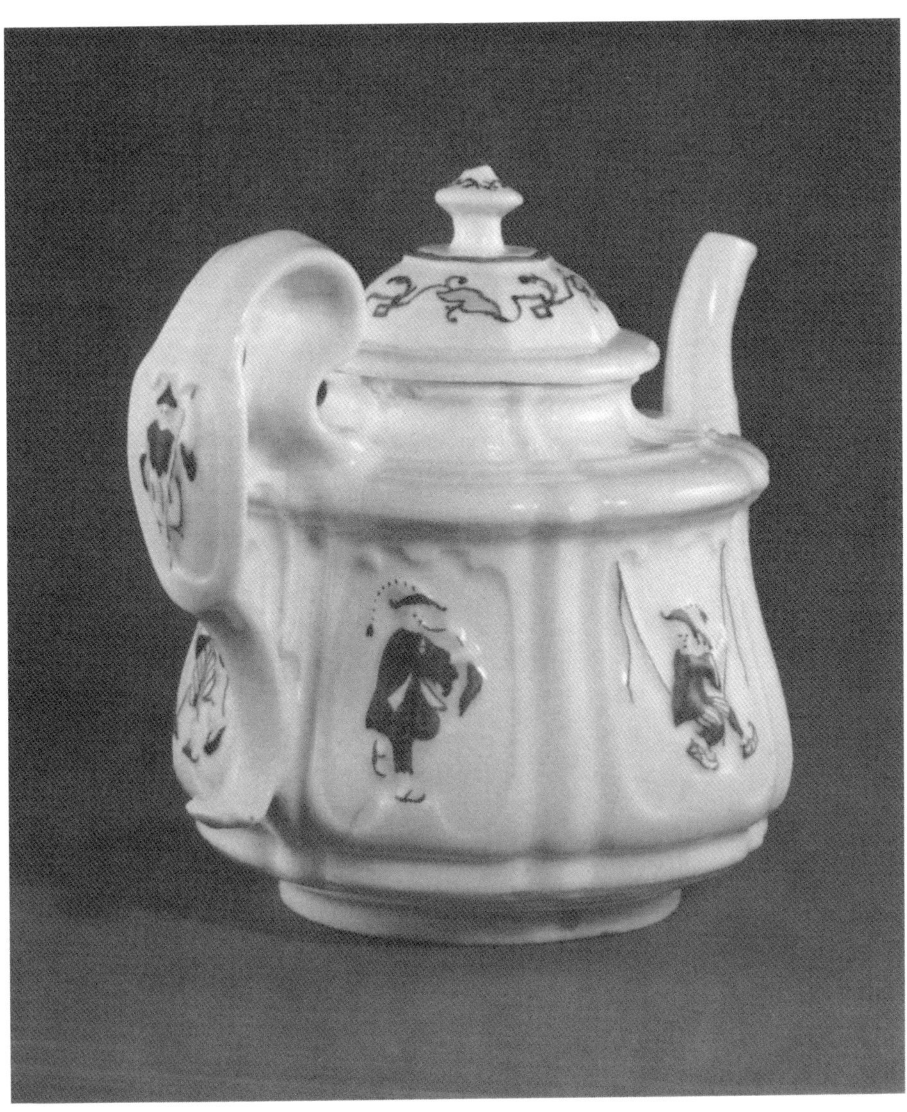

1. *Teapot, Vezzi, 1720–27*

century. Many of these motifs, and the simple linear border designs that frequently accompany them, are very like Du Paquier work, but differ in the undiluted brilliance of coloring in a palette of deep blue, green, brick red, and yellow; by a spirited sketchiness of drawing; and by a tendency to float decoration in undefined space. Pictorial decoration (not represented in the Museum's collection) includes classical, theatrical, and hunting subjects and chinoiseries; these are usually painted in monochrome or gold and may reflect Vezzi's acquaintance with the work of the German *Hausmaler,* or independent porcelain decorators, as he is believed to have visited Augsburg after his stay in Vienna. The names of one or two painters have been noted, but, apart from a single plate in the British Museum signed by Ludovico Ortolani, their work has not been identified.

Vezzi porcelains are generally marked in iron-red enamel with the name of the city (*Venezia*), written out in full or in one of a variety of abbreviated forms, in roman or script letters. A number of unidentified incised marks have also been recorded: as they appear under the glaze they are probably molders' marks.

The factory closed in 1727, largely due to Giovanni Vezzi's financial difficulties. In addition, the Saxon clay was abruptly no longer available. Hunger had left Venice in 1724, and it has been said that on his return to Meissen three years later with news of the Venetian factory, Meissen cut off further supplies of its clay. The premises were destroyed, and no porcelain manufacture is recorded in the region until the middle of the century, when three factories started up at about the same time. The first of these was a short-lived enterprise (1758–1763) whose proprietors, Nathaniel Friedrich Hewelcke and his wife, had been porcelain retailers in Dresden and were victims of the collapse of Meissen during the Seven Years' War. Examples of this factory's production are extremely rare and are not represented in the Museum's collections. In 1762 Pasquale Antonibon (d. 1773), whose father had started a majolica factory in 1728 at Le Nove, northwest of Venice, began producing porcelain there; and in the same year Geminiano Cozzi (1728–1797/8)—who had been associated with Hewelcke—began experimental production in Venice itself. The early history of the two factories is interrelated, as illness caused Antonibon to withdraw from business almost at once, and when he resumed in 1765 Cozzi had received a privilege and opened his factory with the assistance of some of Antonibon's former employees. Le Nove continued under Antonibon's direction until his death in 1773. It is believed that no porcelain was made at Le Nove from then until 1781, when the factory was leased for twenty years to Francesco Parolin. This interrupted history of Le Nove and the relative scarcity of surviving examples make it difficult to gain a clear picture of the factory's development.

At the outset Cozzi and Le Nove used the same kaolin from Vicenza, and in addition to this correspondence of material there are occasional resemblances in color and in painting styles. The paste was quite gray, and pieces from the two factories are sometimes almost indistinguishable, but the surface of Cozzi pieces inclines to a slight texture and the glaze is more brilliant.

Small tablewares, ornamental vases, and sculpture were produced in both places. At Cozzi a common decoration of cups and saucers was an architectural landscape with or without figures, to which a coat of arms was occasionally added. Such decoration was painted in a somewhat muddy palette in which purple, russet, green, and brownish yellow predominated. Clusters of fruit and flowers appear in the work of both Cozzi and Le Nove in similar light palettes of iron red, yellow, green, and purple, those of Cozzi being distinguished by a greater attention to drawing.

The decoration of Cozzi tablewares appears to have been more varied than that of Le Nove, encompassing enframed harbor scenes in the Meissen manner, armorials, luxuriant floral ornament, rococo chinoiseries, and oriental export patterns. At both factories the models developed from heavy molded forms of baroque inspiration to lighter, more rococo ones reflecting the rapidly increasing international influence of Sèvres. Sculpture played an important role at Cozzi, and examples in the Museum's collection comprehend the factory's wide repertoire. A taste for the grotesque is evident in the exaggerated expressions and gestures of dwarfs and theatrical figures (3) and dwarflike children with heavy round heads; the groups are often arranged in a circular composition around a central tree trunk (4). This circular form also occurs in

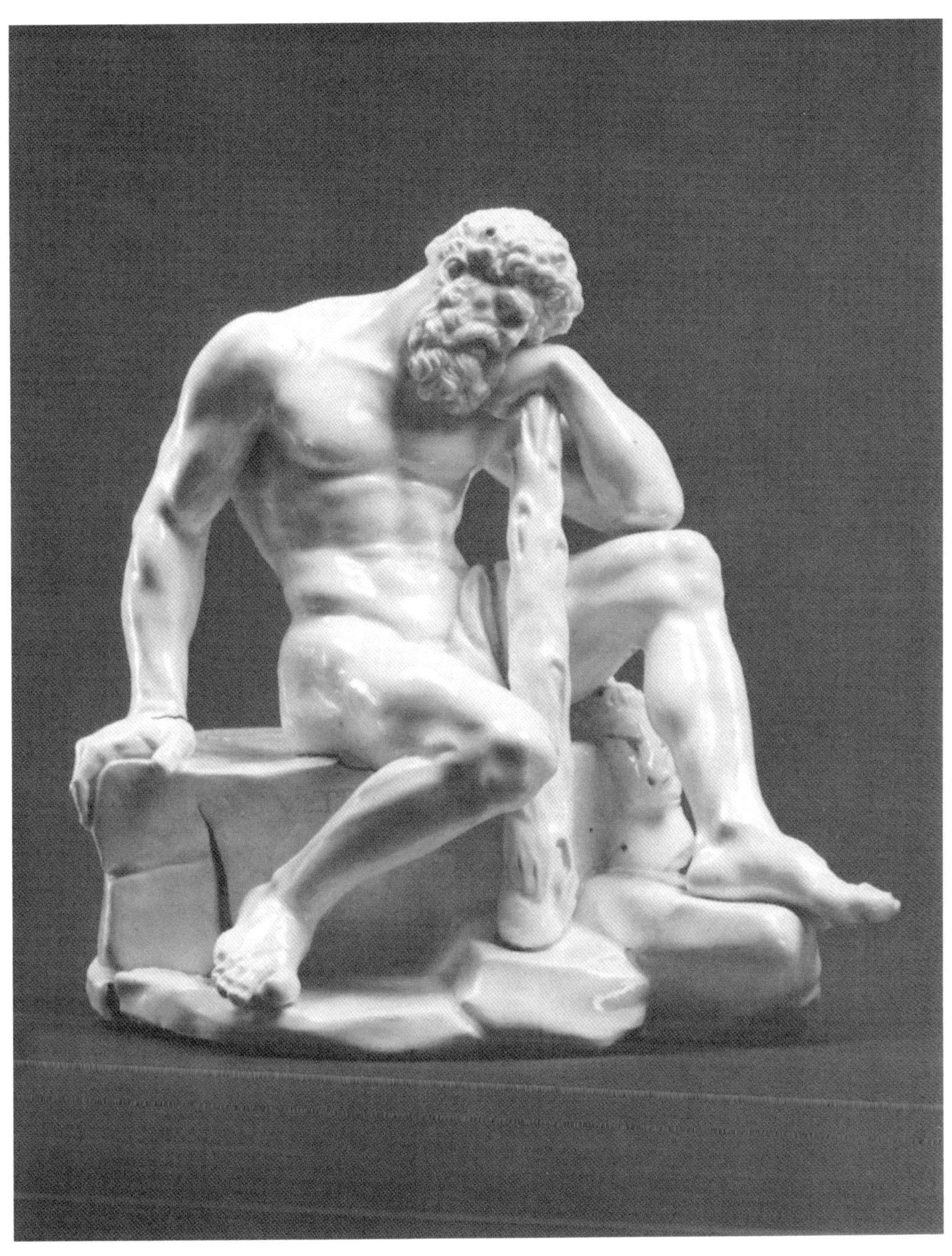

2. *Hercules.* Possibly LeNove, 1765–70

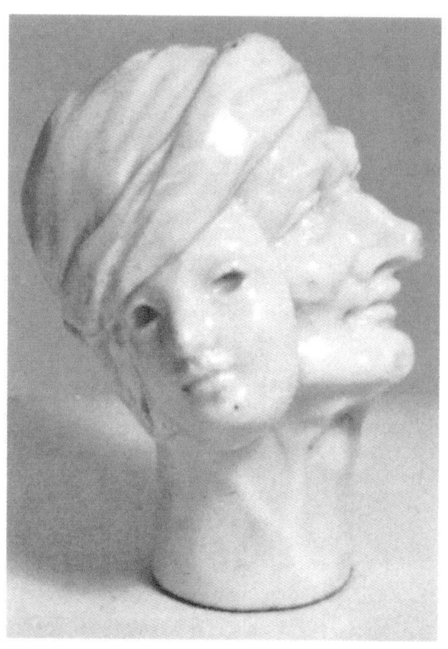

3. *Cane handle.* Cozzi, about 1770

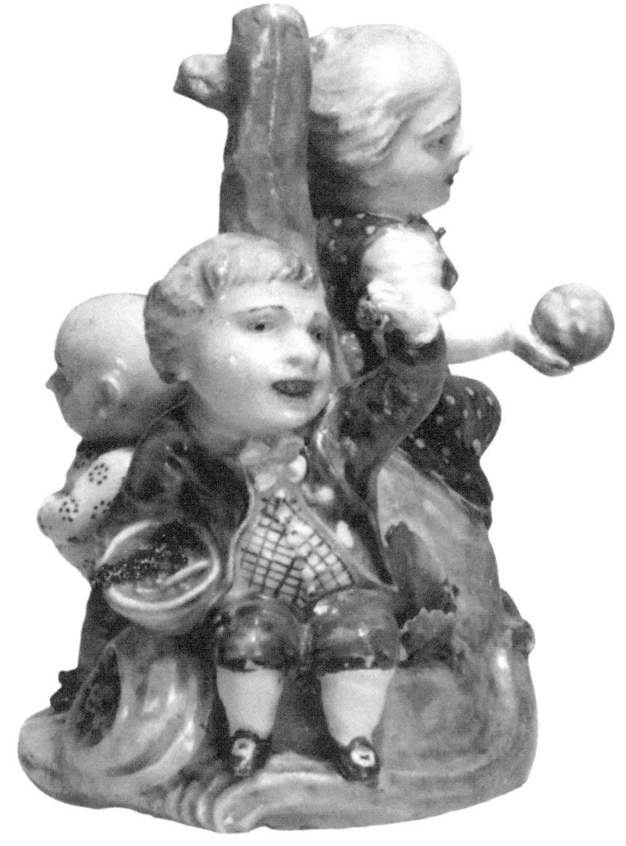

4. *Three children.* Cozzi, about 1775

small-scale mythological and fountain groups. A popular blanc de chine export figure of Pu t'ai, the god of happiness, was copied at Cozzi, as at other European factories, in brightly colored versions. Cozzi sculpture was for the most part left undecorated, although the smaller genre groups are to be found painted in a subdued range of greens, browns, and blues. Quite atypical of Cozzi work, and achieving a high level of sculptural importance, is a relief portrait of the actor Carlo Bertinazzi (5), executed with great verve and crispness. The Cozzi sculptures are clearly by different modelers, and the names of several are known; there is, however, insufficient evidence on which to attempt specific attributions. The tablewares of Cozzi and Le Nove were generally marked, one with an anchor with a double ring painted haphazardly in iron red, the other with a star formed of three intersecting lines. The latter is found in both iron-red and blue enamel. Sculpture produced at both factories was unmarked.

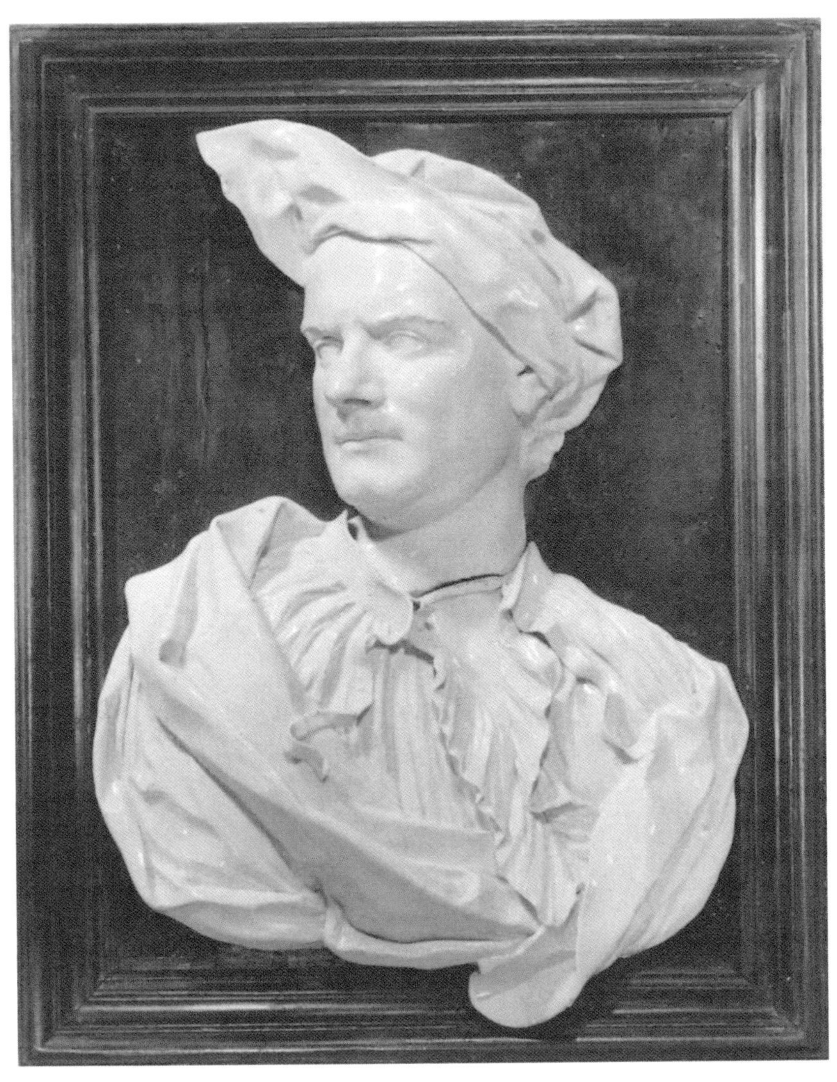

5. *Relief portrait of Carlo Antonio Bertinazzi* (1710–1783). Cozzi, about 1770

DOCCIA

With the end of the Medici enterprise in 1587 there was no porcelain manufacture in Florence until 1737, when Marchese Carlo Ginori (1702–1757), a man of an inquiring and scientific turn of mind, began experimenting with the composition of porcelain in his Florentine palace. In that same year Tuscany, hitherto an appanage of the dukes of Lorraine, became attached to Austria through the marriage of the then duke, Francis, to Maria Theresa. Ginori promptly went to Vienna to pay his respects to the empress, and there he met and hired Karl Wendelin Anreiter von Zirnfeld (1702–1747), a *Hausmaler* who was certainly familiar with, and may also have worked for, the Vienna factory founded by Claude Du Paquier. With the assistance of Anreiter and of the kilnmaster Giorgio delle Torri, a former Du Paquier employee, and advice on glaze and colors from Giovanni Vezzi in Venice, Ginori formally established his factory at Doccia, near Florence, in 1737, receiving an exclusive privilege for the manufacture of porcelain in Tuscany in 1741.

Ginori's most pressing concern was his material. Kaolin is not a clay of uniform whiteness, and the local supply on which Ginori depended was far from the pure white of the Saxon clay used at Meissen. There is some variation in the paste from time to time, indicating that Ginori experimented with several formulas, but with few exceptions the result—known as *masso bastardo*—was a heavy, rather crude, and distinctly gray body. About 1770 the factory introduced a tin glaze to produce a white surface, and this continued in sporadic use for some time.

What Doccia lacked in delicacy of material and technique was more than made up for by vigor and imagination of design. Tablewares were boldly modeled, with shaped profiles, frequent use of animal-form spouts or handles, heavy moldings, and decoration in relief, all evoking a massiveness associated with silversmiths' work. The coloring is strongly reminiscent of the Du Paquier palette, in which purple, iron red, yellow, and green predominated. Viennese influence is also found in some of the flower painting, as on a set of platters and dishes depicting Turks (6), but other decorative schemes were quite original to Doccia. Unique among eighteenth-century decoration was Doccia's stenciled underglaze blue (7), a technique that dates from the first years of the factory and reached its height about 1745. The patterns were generally of orientalizing flowers, and the Museum's example is conspicuous for its unusually white body and brilliant glaze. Another characteristic oriental design, of which an example is in the Museum's collection, is a well-known one described in 1757 as *a tulipano*, which features a dramatically shaded iron-red tuliplike flower of a type also found on Chinese porcelains of the period.

Ginori's great interest was in sculpture, and even some tablewares are treated as bas-reliefs, with elaborate, crowded mythological compositions. In 1737 Ginori had engaged the sculptor Gaspero Bruschi (ca. 1701–1780), who was appointed master of modelers in 1742 and remained at Doccia until his death. Bruschi was the author of a number of original models, but a significant part of his work lay in the production of sculptures cast from molds made from wax models of Florentine bronzes of the late

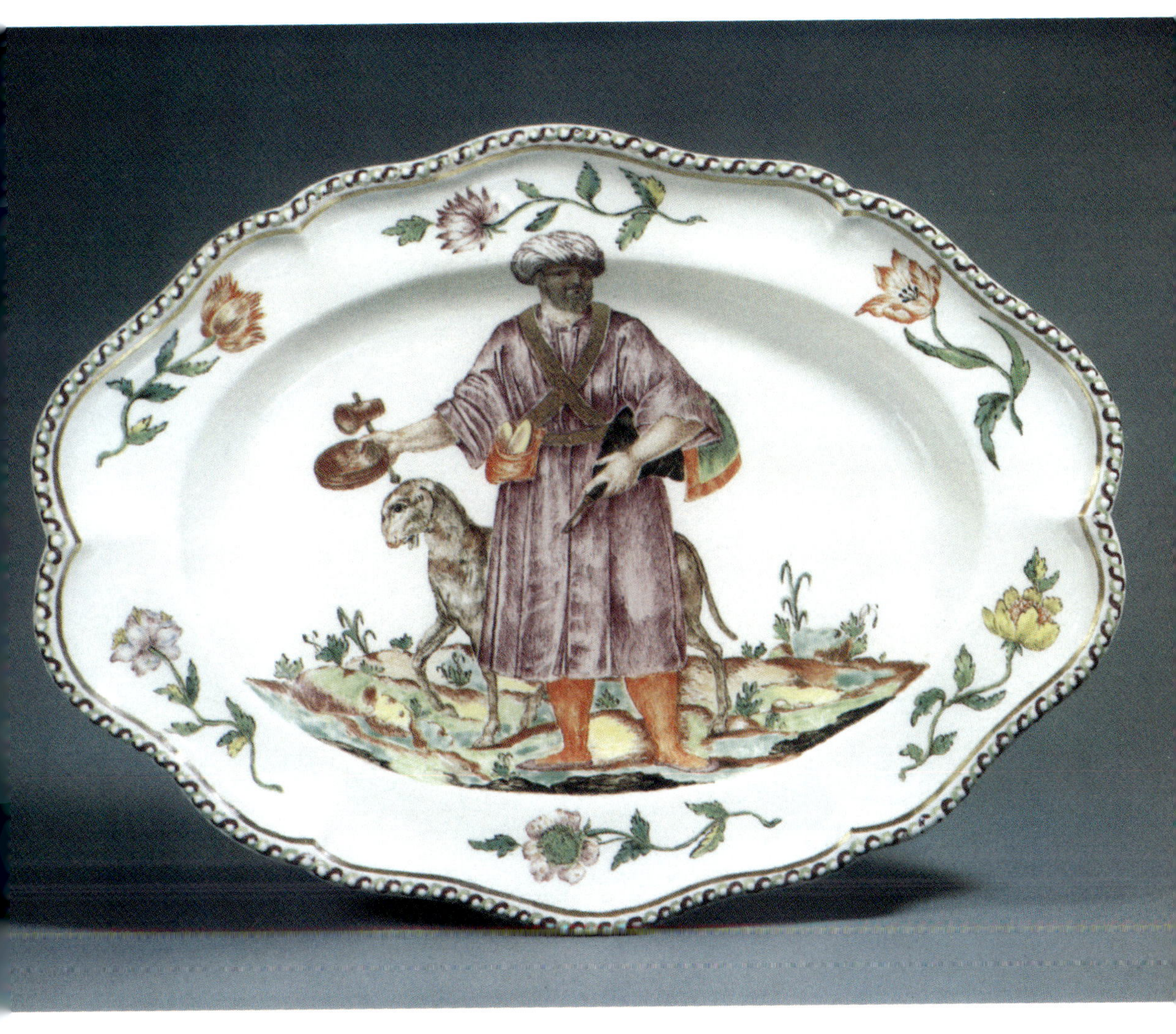

6. *Platter.* Doccia, about 1740

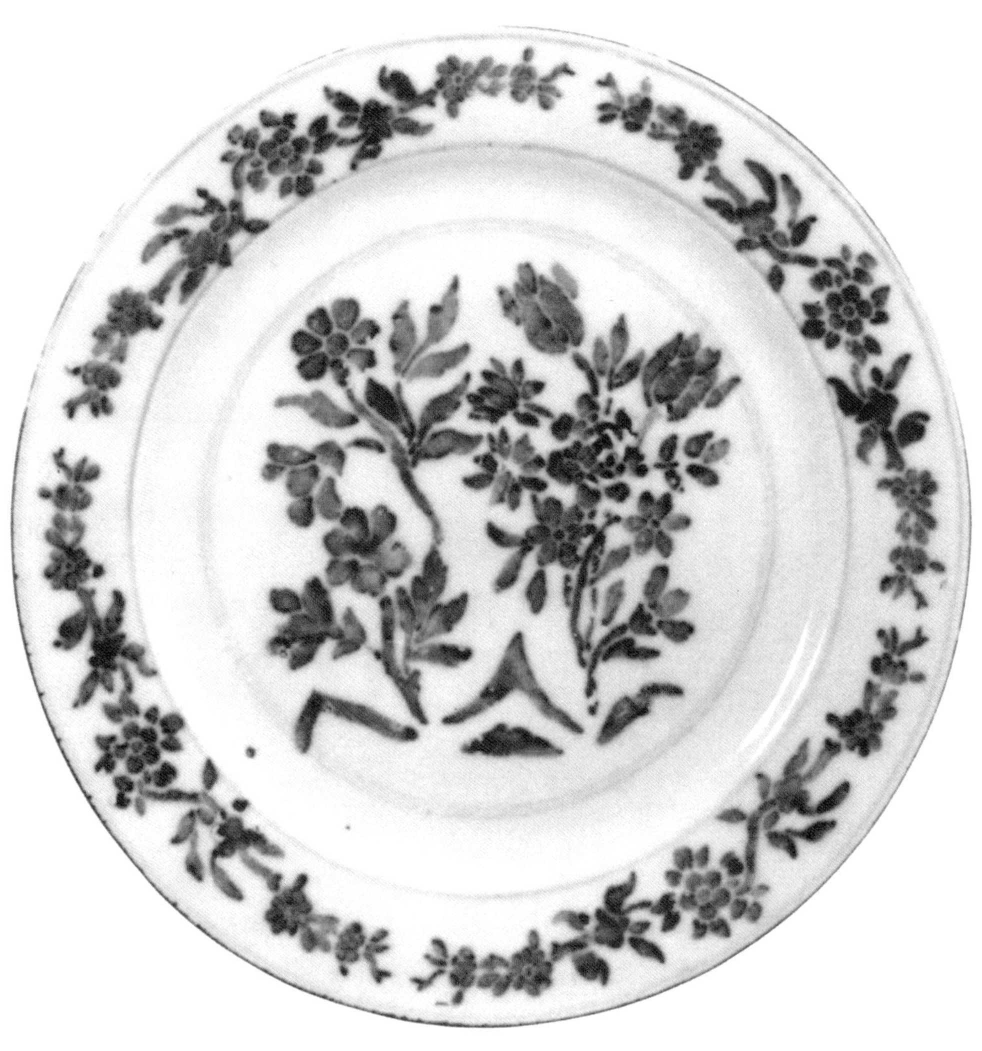

7. *Plate with underglaze blue stenciled decoration.* Doccia, 1740–45

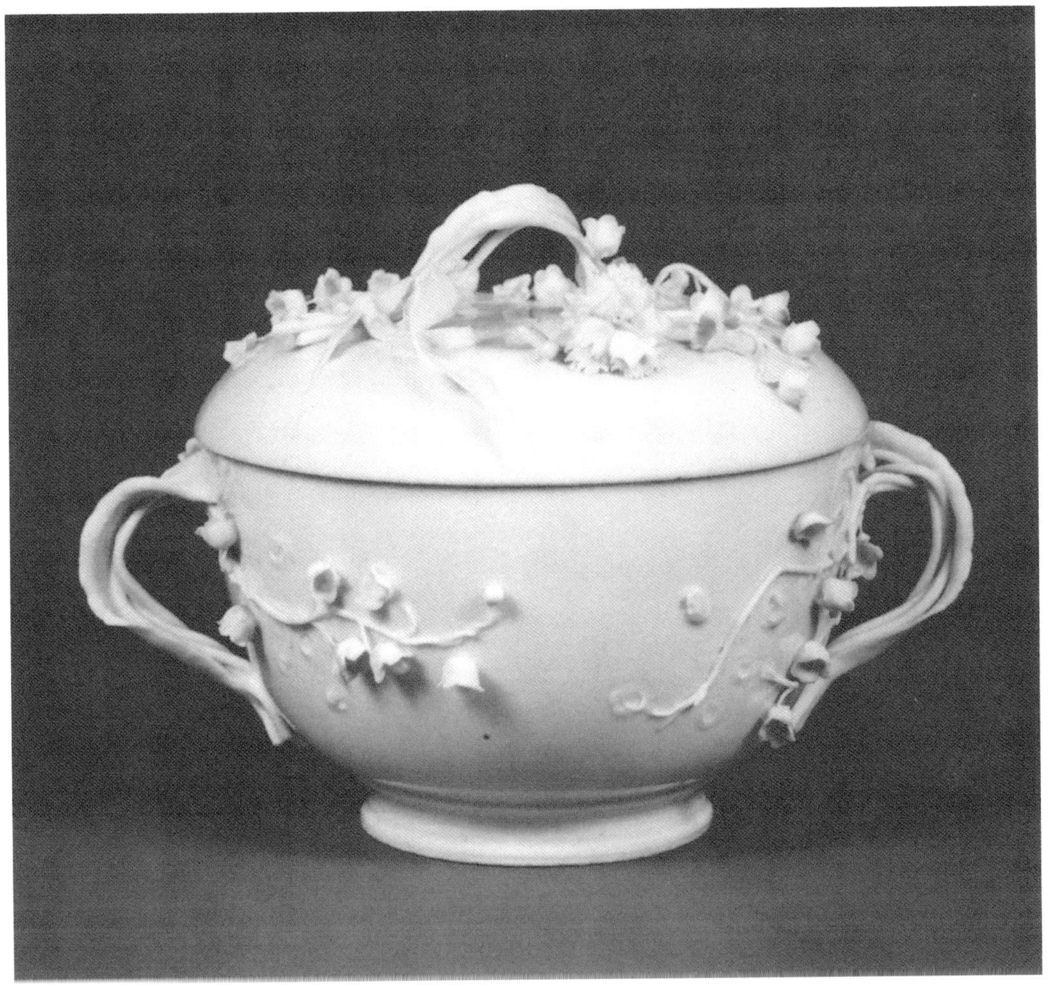

8. *Covered bowl* (*écuelle*). Doccia, 1750–55

seventeenth and early eighteenth centuries. Ginori had amassed a large collection of these specially for conversion to porcelain, and among the more than 150 works were models by Giuseppe Piamontini (1664–1742), Massimiliano Soldani-Benzi (1656–1740), and Giovanni Battista Foggini (1652–1725). Many were very large, such as a Pietà by Soldani over three feet in length, cast in porcelain in an eighteen-piece mold. It was an experiment that recalls Meissen's early production of enormous figures of animals and birds that stretched the capabilities of porcelain almost beyond its limits and was characteristic of Ginori's adventurous drive.

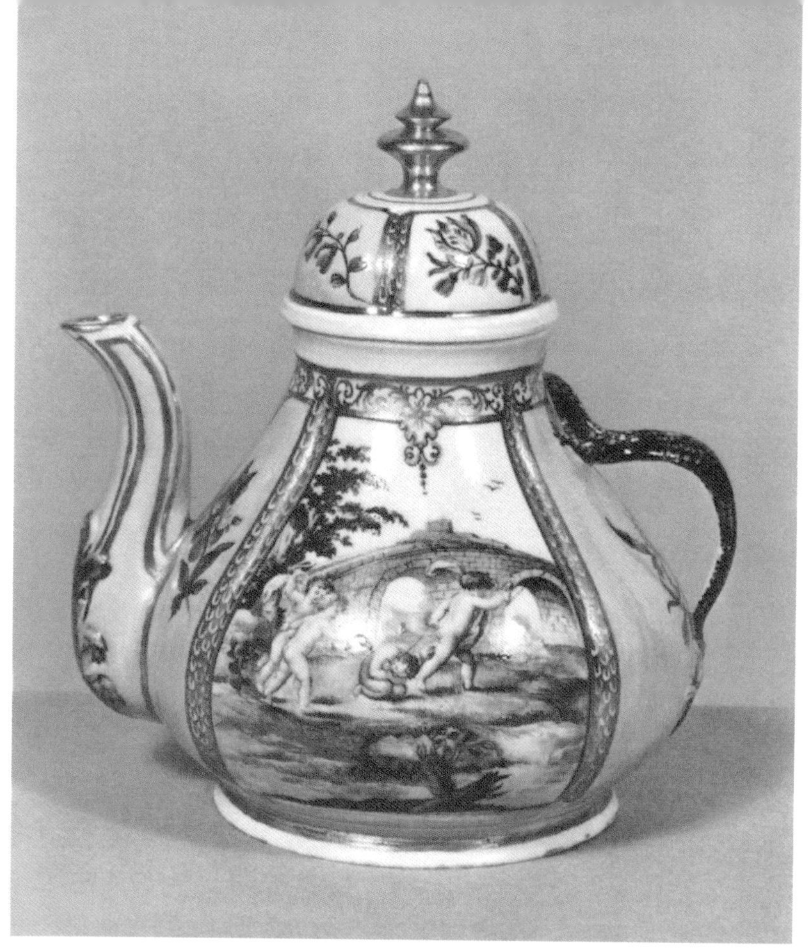

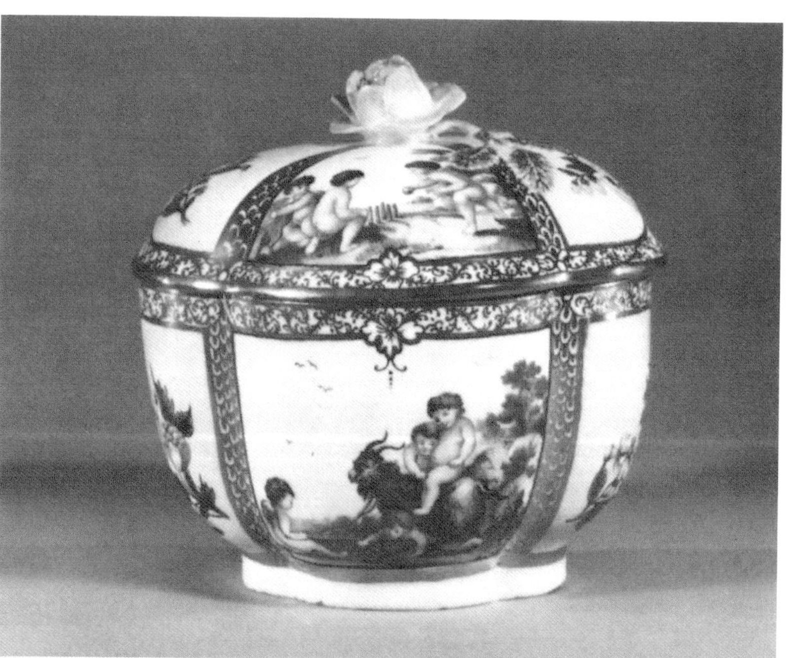

9. *Teapot and sugar bowl.* Doccia, 1750–55

After Ginori's death the factory, under the proprietorship of his son Lorenzo, turned to more conventional figures on a smaller scale. Among examples in the Museum's collection are figures of Turks after engravings first published in 1714 (10), a spirited dancing girl copied from a model of about 1748 by J. J. Kändler at Meissen, and figures of Winter (11) and Spring after small ivories by Balthasar Permoser (1651–1732) then in the Ginori collection. In all these smaller figures the paste is characteristically gray and, when colored, painted in an almost harsh palette of puce, iron red, green, and lemon yellow. Flesh tones were indicated by patches of iron-red stippling, and black stippling was used for eyes and eyebrows. The figures occur in variant models and with two types of bases, one square with dark marbling, succeeded by one vigorously scrolled and usually colored puce. Doccia figures were unmarked, and it was only after about 1780 that a regular factory mark of a star (from the Ginori coat of arms) was introduced for use on tablewares.

Doccia is the only Italian factory to have continued operation since the eighteenth century. In 1896 it was acquired by the Société Richard and since then has been known as Richard-Ginori.

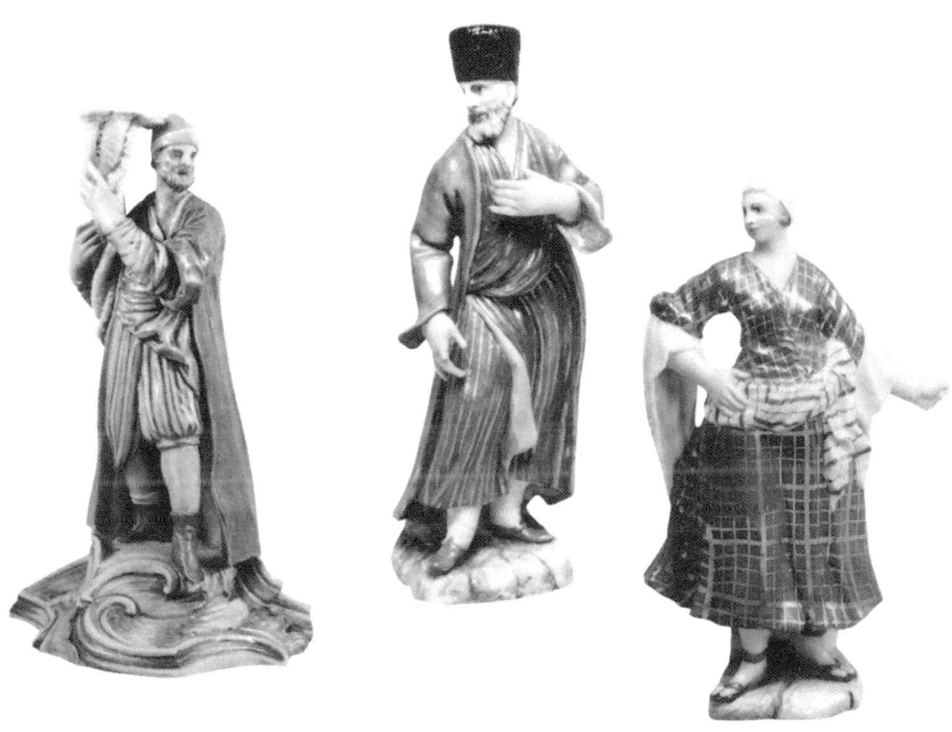

10. *Three Turks.* Doccia, 1760–70

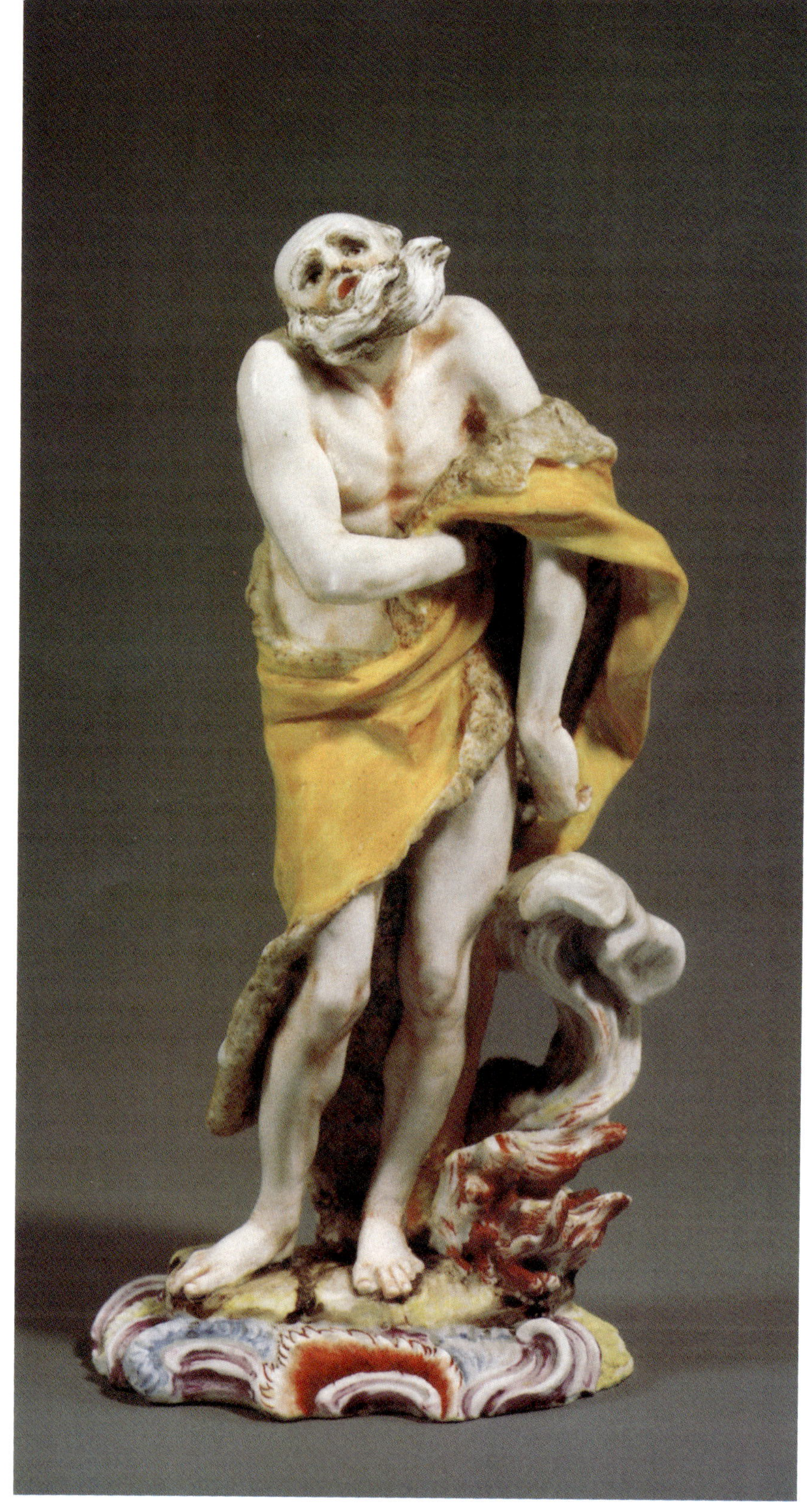

11. *Winter.* Doccia, about 1770

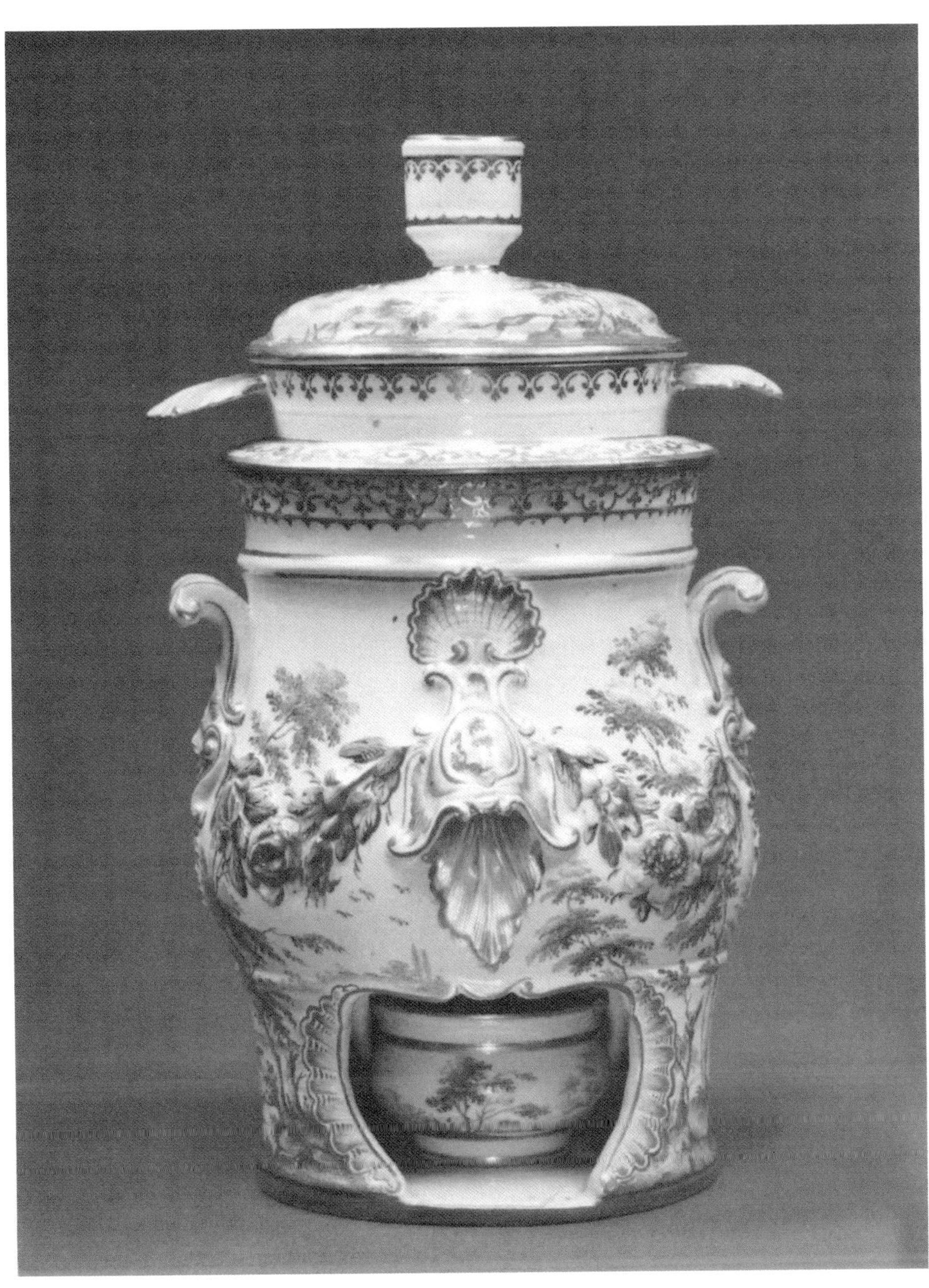

12. *Food warmer.* Doccia, about 1770

CAPODIMONTE

Experiments in porcelain manufacture in Naples began about 1740 at the instigation of Charles, king of the Two Sicilies. Charles's wife, Maria Amalia, was a granddaughter of Augustus the Strong, and her dowry is reputed to have included seventeen Meissen table services, which may well have been a factor in the Bourbon king's decision to promote a factory of his own. He was also well aware of Ginori's Doccia enterprise, as he attempted (unsuccessfully) to lure Karl Wendelin Anreiter and his son from Florence to Naples. Ultimately, Charles engaged Livio and Gaetano Schepers as arcanists, while his chief modeler throughout the duration of the factory was Giuseppe Gricci (1700–1770). The factory was formally established in 1743 on the grounds of the royal palace at Capodimonte on a hillside outside Naples.

The material developed by the Schepers brothers—mostly by Gaetano—was of a particularly clear warm white covered with a mildly lustrous glaze. The coloring of both tablewares and figures was generally in clear and bright hues of blue, green, yellow ocher, orange, red, and puce, imparting a freshness and lightness to the factory's work.

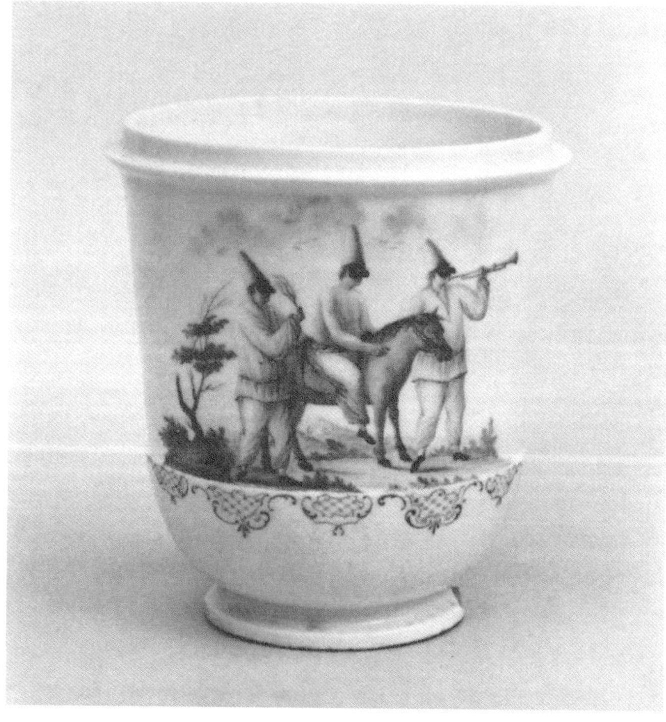

13. *Vase.* Capodimonte, about 1750

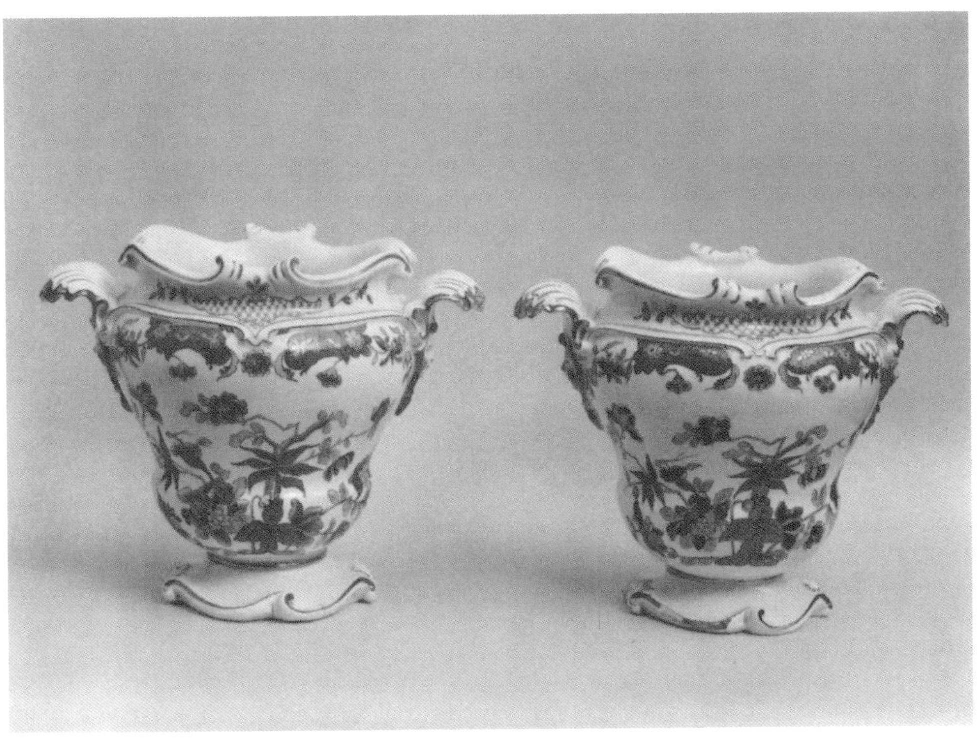

14. *Pair of vases.* Capodimonte, 1755–59

The first half-dozen years of Capodimonte are well documented, and during that period its production included tea and coffee sets, ornamental vases, snuffboxes and cane handles, and figures. A number of the tablewares give evidence of Meissen or Viennese influence, either in the baroque character of their models or in their scheme of decoration, which often incorporated simplified lace or strapwork borders. In its painted decoration, however, Capodimonte developed a style of its own, perhaps introduced by Giovanni Caselli (1698–1752), who from 1743 until his death directed the factory's painting workshop. Pictorial compositions were built up by gradations of very fine stippling in which much use was made of soft grays and browns (13). Quite different was the factory's oriental manner, which was highly stylized and brilliant in palette (14), culminating in an entire room made for the palace at Portici (and now in Capodimonte) of molded and painted porcelain panels alive with flowers, exotic foliage, monkeys, and Orientals.

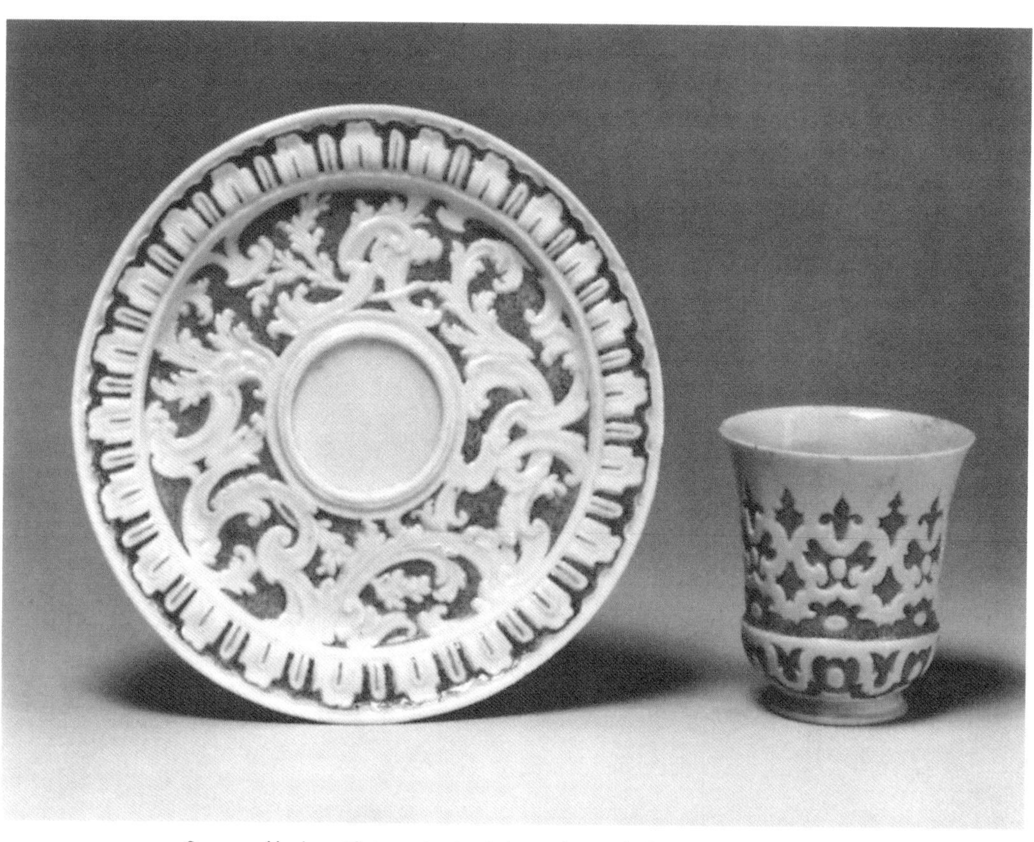

15. *Saucer and beaker with decoration in relief on pink ground.* Capodimonte, about 1743

Among early Capodimonte models are a cup and saucer with ornate carving recalling the gem cutter's craft and undoubtedly the work of one of the *intagliatori* employed by the factory in 1743 (15). Also introduced in the first year of the factory's existence was a model of snuffbox that was to prove especially popular: of shell form, its surface composed of numerous varieties of shells and marine plant life modeled in low relief (16). It was the invention of Giuseppe Gricci, to whom almost all of the factory's sculptural work has been assigned.

Of Florentine birth, Gricci went to Naples in 1738 as sculptor to the king, and it was presumably from him that Charles learned of the Anreiters and the newly founded Doccia factory. Gricci's versatility is evident from the work attributed to him in Capodimonte's first two years: from 1743 to 1745 he is cited as the modeler of large religious figures and groups, royal portraits, tablewares, snuffboxes, and such secular sculptures as putti, commedia-dell'arte characters, and poor people. Of the very large output of figures only one bears Gricci's signature. It is a figure of the mourning Virgin (17) from a Crucifixion group modeled with a masterly sense of controlled drama, its sculptural intensity undisturbed by painted decoration.

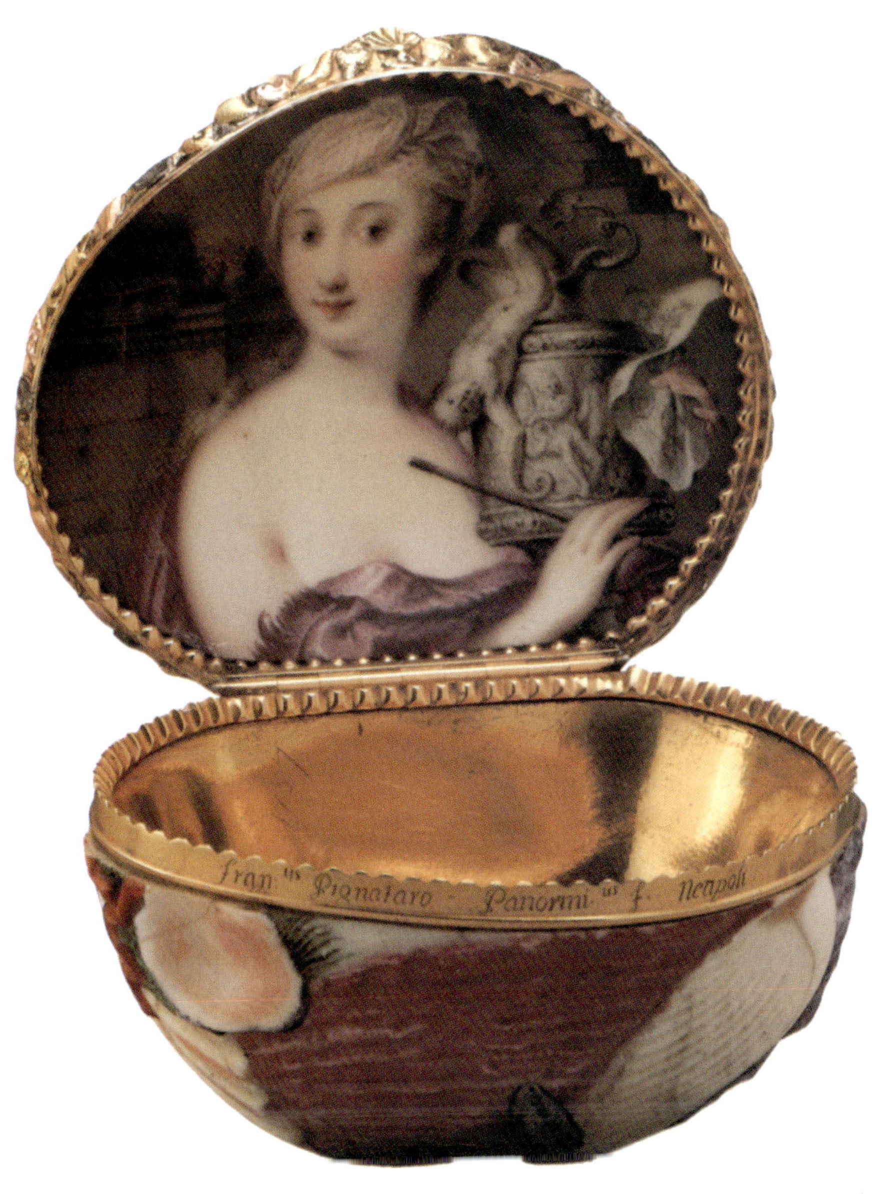

16. *Snuffbox with gold rims.* Capodimonte, about 1745

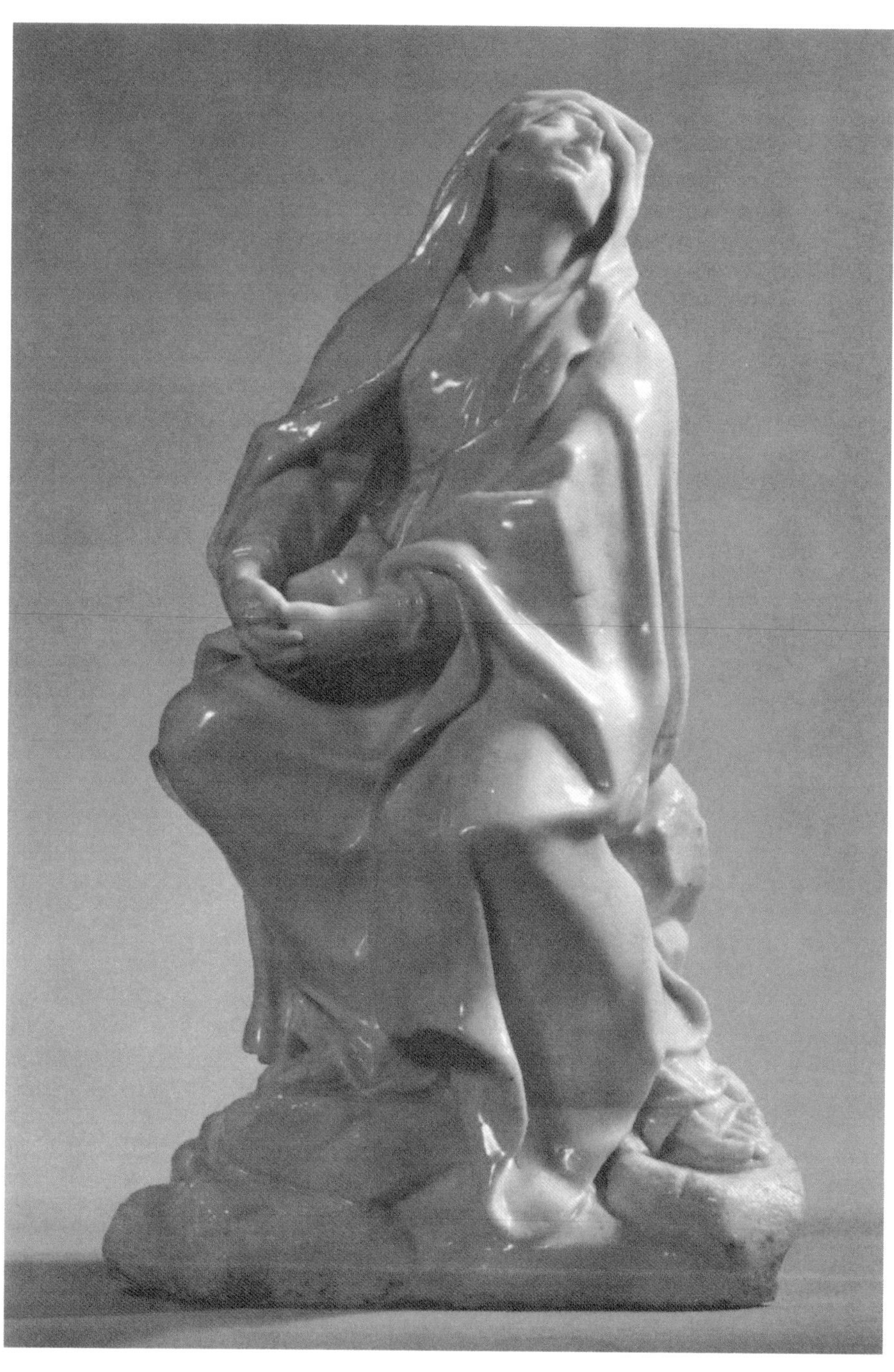

17. *Mater Dolorosa.* Capodimonte, about 1744

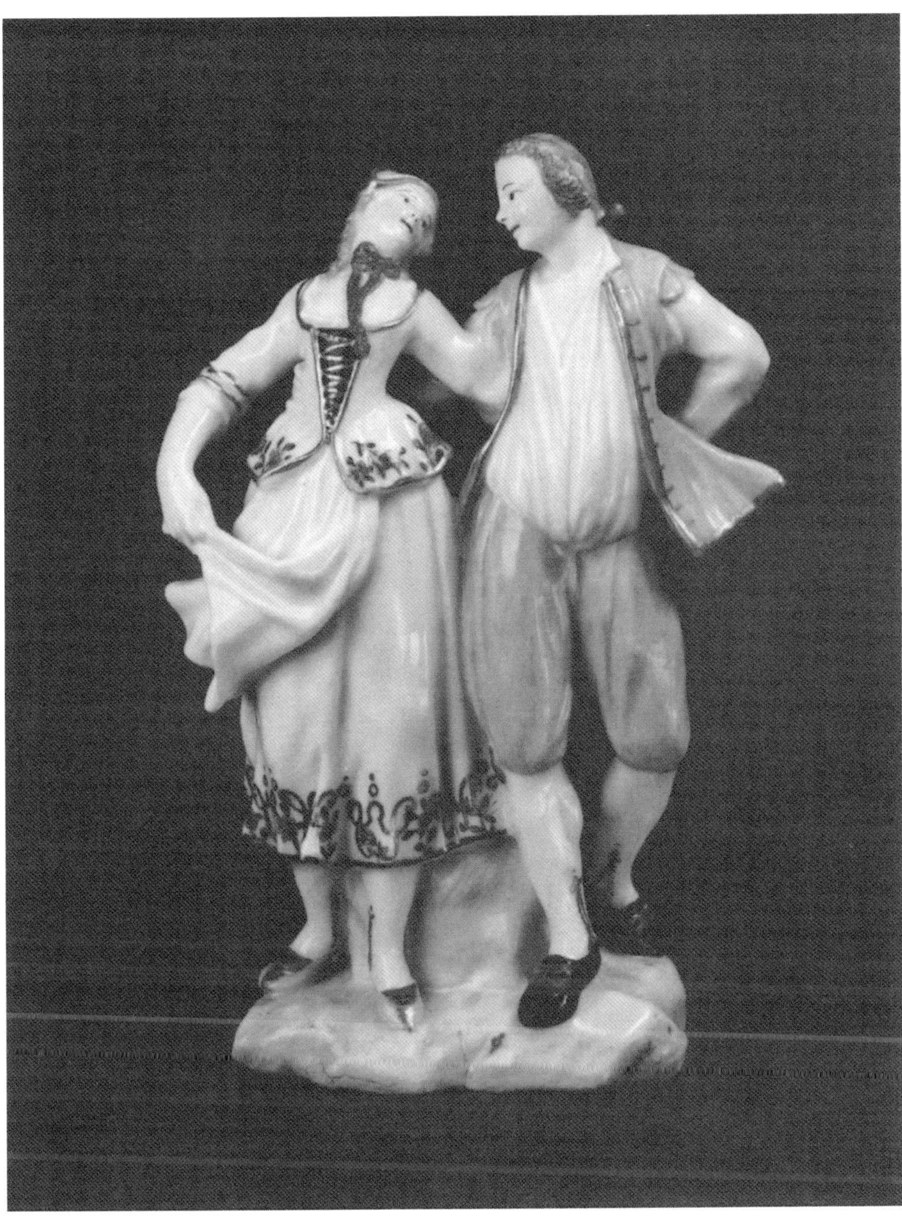

18. *Dancing Couple.* Capodimonte, 1750–55

Reference to figures of *poveri* in 1744 has led to the attribution to Gricci of a large number of figures and groups of street vendors, actors, and lovers (18). As there were by 1755 five modelers working under him, and as the output of these figures was prodigious, it is unlikely that all should be considered Gricci's work, but they have in common a consistently benign appreciation of different situations and classes of society, and certain stylistic mannerisms as well. Chief among these are exceptionally small heads, wide hands and feet, and restrained painting of both features and costume. A prevailing expression of worried good humor is conveyed by coal-speck eyes and short, swiftly drawn eyebrows; and details of costume are often kept to a minimum, defined by a simple band of trimming or a slight airy pattern rendered in bright colors or gold, creating an exceptionally harmonious rhythm between the white porcelain and its decoration (19). A number of figures were left in the white, and some of these, regrettably, have been decorated in recent times. The modeling was generally rather simple and blocklike, but with an unerring eye for pose and gesture and, in the narrative groups, for the dramatic tension between the personae (21, 22). The bases

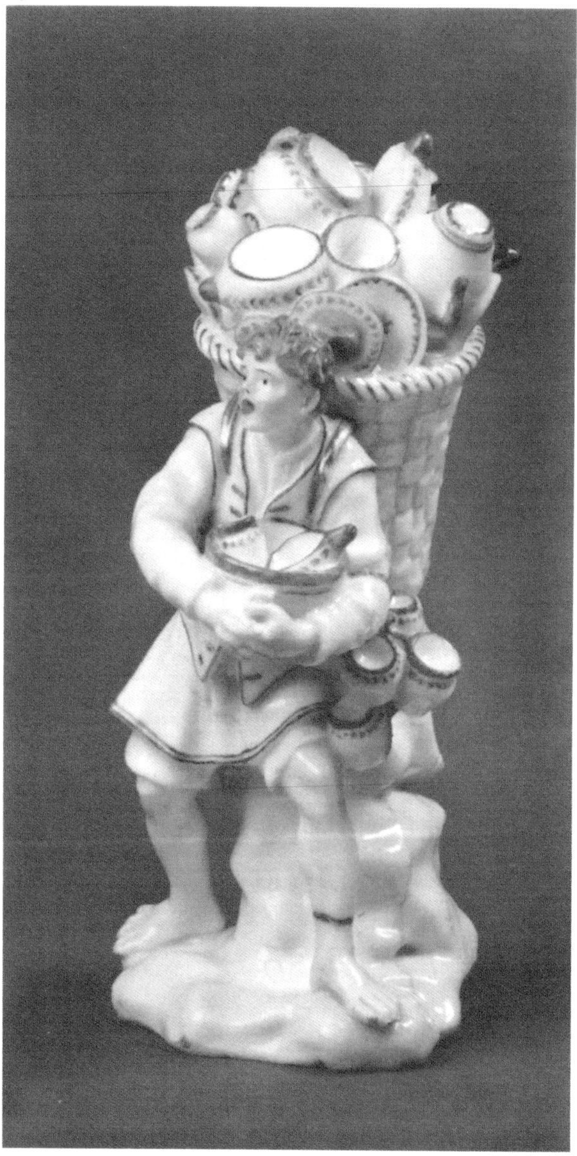

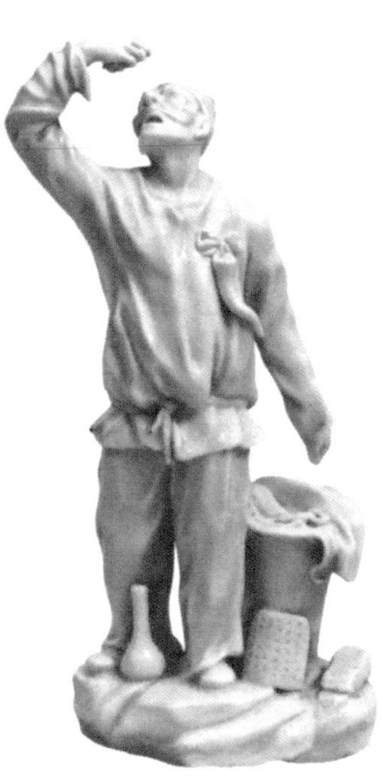

20. *Pulcinella*. Capodimonte, 1745–50

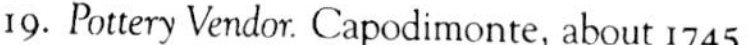

19. *Pottery Vendor*. Capodimonte, about 1745

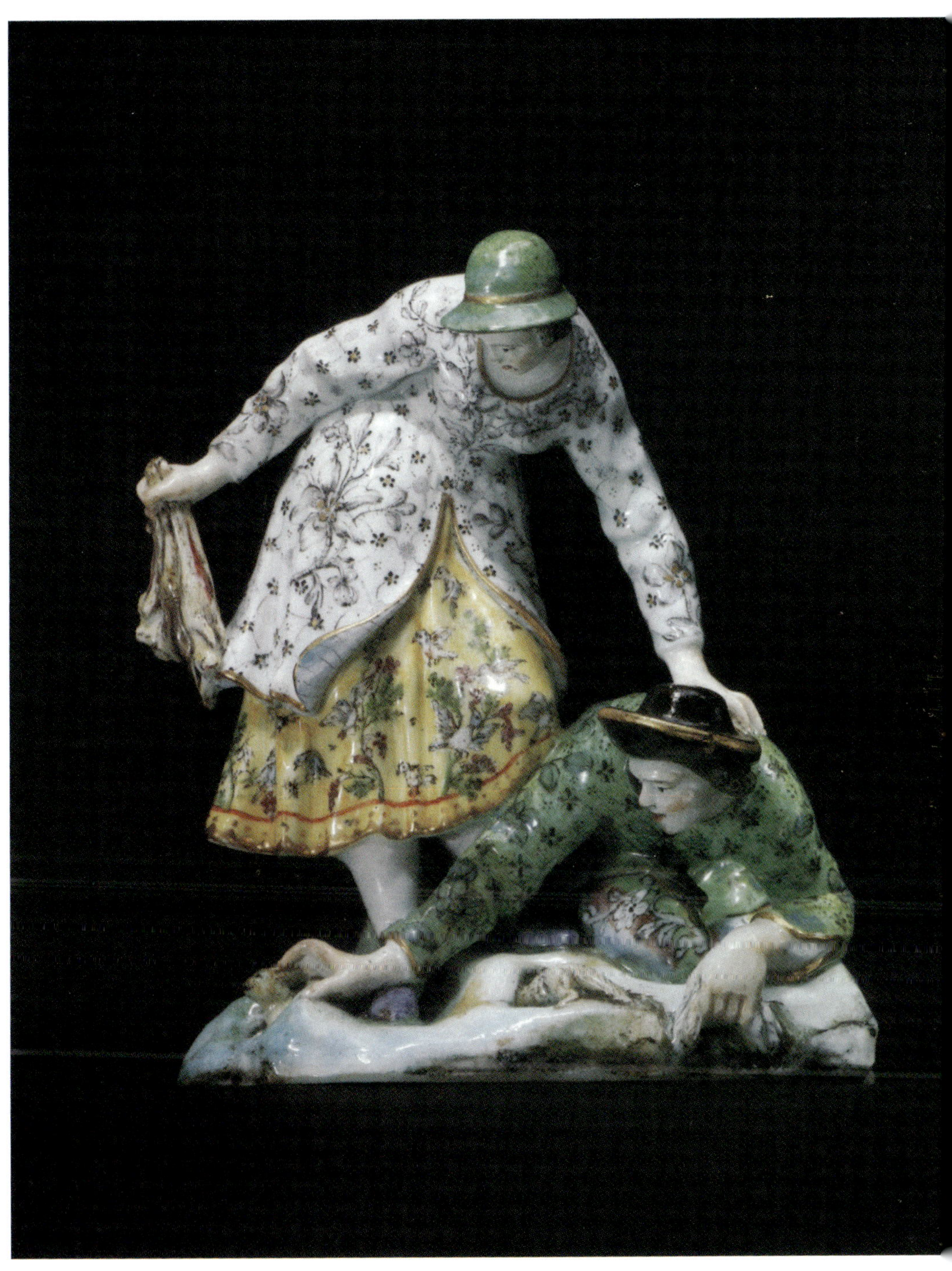

21. *The Rabbit Catchers.* Capodimonte, 1755–59

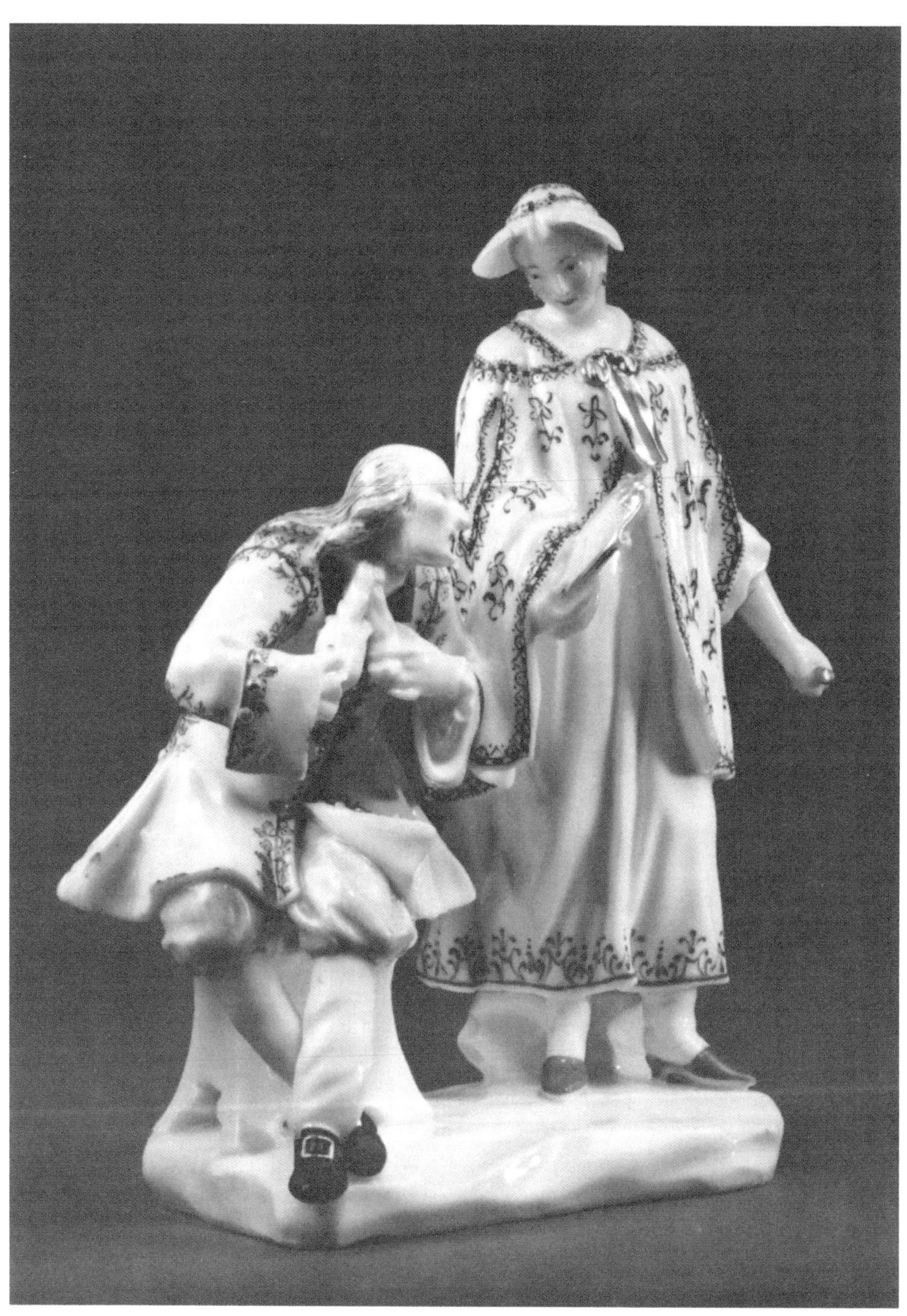

22. *Old Man Dressing*. Capodimonte, about 1750

are of irregular mound form with bumpy rocklike protuberances. Variations on this basic formula occur, but whether they are due to a change in Gricci's own style or to other hands cannot be determined. The figures become proportionally more balanced, their scale is somewhat enlarged, and there is a greater use of areas of monochrome in subdued pastel tones. A small group of sculptures is characterized by a green-tinged glaze of varying intensity, becoming at its most extreme an outright turquoise. As there is little information concerning Capodimonte after about 1750, it is not possible to determine the sequence (or simultaneity) of these features, but some recur later in Madrid and may thus date from the last years of the factory.

In 1759 Charles succeeded to the Spanish throne as Charles III, and in October of that year he removed his porcelain factory from Capodimonte to the royal palace of Buen Retiro on the outskirts of Madrid. Accompanying him were Gricci, Gaetano Schepers, and some forty other factory personnel, together with equipment and nearly five tons of paste. This transfer of the entire works resulted in a continuity of material and style that makes it difficult to distinguish between late Capodimonte and early Buen Retiro porcelains. The difficulty is compounded by the continued use in Spain of the Capodimonte factory mark of a fleur-de-lis. At both factories it was painted in underglaze blue, but on Capodimonte figures it is also encountered impressed within a circle.

In Naples itself there was no further manufacture of porcelain for fifteen years. The factory premises at Capodimonte were destroyed and, when Charles's son and successor, Ferdinand IV of Naples, decided to revive porcelain making, he built an entirely new factory. It was situated first at Portici and, from 1773, on the grounds of the royal palace and was active until 1806. Ferdinand's Royal Factory was one of many established in Italy toward the end of the eighteenth century. Starting in a spirit of neoclassicism, their productions introduce the history of nineteenth-century porcelain.

1. **Teapot.** Hard paste. H. 4¾ in. (12.1 cm.)
Marks: *Ven:a* in red; *Nf* incised
Venice, Vezzi, 1720–27
Rogers Fund, 1906
06.362ab
The cover is not original to the body, but is by Vezzi and is contemporaneous.

2. **Hercules.** Hard paste. H. 8¾ in. (22.2 cm.)
Possibly Le Nove, ca. 1765–70
The Charles E. Sampson Memorial Fund, 1981
1981.412
The paste and glaze are very similar to that found in Cozzi sculpture, but the subject and modeling are quite different.

3. **Cane handle.** Hard paste. H. 3 in. (7.6 cm.)
Venice, Cozzi, ca. 1770
Gift of Irwin Untermyer, 1964
64.101.335

4. **Three children.** Hard paste. H. 4⁵⁄₁₆ in. (11 cm.)
Venice, Cozzi, ca. 1775
Bequest of R. Thornton Wilson, in memory of his wife, Florence Ellsworth Wilson, 1977
1977.216.19

5. **Relief portrait of Carlo Antonio Bertinazzi (1710–1783).** Hard paste. H. 18¼ in. (46.4 cm.)
Venice, Cozzi, ca. 1770
Gift of R. Thornton Wilson, 1966, in memory of James R. Rorimer
66.92
Bertinazzi, born in Turin and educated for an army career, turned to acting and became the most celebrated of the eighteenth-century Harlequins in the commedia dell'arte. In 1741 he joined the Italian Comedy troupe in Paris, where he remained until his death.

6. **Platter.** Hybrid paste. L. 12½ in. (31.8 cm.)
Decoration attributed to Karl Wendelin Anreiter von Zirnfeld
Doccia, ca. 1740
Rogers Fund, 1906
06.372b
One of three platters in the Metropolitan Museum from a dispersed set of eighteen platters and two plates depicting figures in Turkish costumes after watercolors by Jacopo Ligozzi (1547–1627).

7. **Plate with underglaze blue stenciled decoration.** Hard paste. Diam. 9⅛ in. (23.2 cm.)
Doccia, 1740–45
The Charles E. Sampson Memorial Fund, 1979
1979.445.3

8. **Covered bowl** (*écuelle*). Hard paste. W. with handles 6½ in. (16.5 cm.)
Doccia, 1750–55
The Charles E. Sampson Memorial Fund, 1979
1979.445.2ab

9. **Teapot and sugar bowl.** Hard paste. H. 7 in. (17.8 cm.), 4⁹⁄₁₆ in. (11.6 cm.)
Doccia, 1750–55
Gift of James A. Lewis, 1946
46.103ab
The Charles E. Sampson Memorial Fund, 1969
69.118ab
Part of a tea service painted with scenes from *Les jeux et plaisirs de l'enfance,* a set of fifty-two engravings published in 1657 by Claudine Bouzonnet-Stella (1627–1697) after compositions by her uncle, Jacques Stella (ca. 1596–1657). Shown on the teapot is pl. 30, *La poire.* Other pieces from the service in the Metropolitan Museum are two cups and saucers (1971.191.1,2 and 1971.233.1,2).

10. **Three Turks.** Hard paste. H. 6⅞ in. (17.5 cm.), 5½ in. (14 cm.), 5⅝ in. (14.3 cm.)
Models attributed to Gaspero Bruschi (working 1737–80)
Doccia, 1760–70
Rogers Fund, 1906
06.397,396,390
From a series of figures based on illustrations in *Recueil de cent estampes représentant differentes nations du Levant*, 1714, a collection of engravings after paintings commissioned by Comte Charles Ferriol, French ambassador to Constantinople. In some versions the figures were modified to incorporate candleholders.

11. **Winter.** Hard paste. H. 7¾ in. (19.7 cm.)
Doccia, ca. 1770
The Charles E. Sampson Memorial Fund, 1972
1972.46
One of four Seasons from a set of ivory figures by Balthasar Permoser owned by Carlo Ginori and mentioned in 1757.

12. **Food warmer.** Hard paste. H. 10 in. (25.4 cm.)
Doccia, ca. 1770
The Lesley and Emma Sheafer Collection, bequest of Emma A. Sheafer, 1973
1974.356.541
Candleholder (original to the warmer but acquired separately):
Rogers Fund, 1976
1976.98
The piece combines the functions of a warmer (*réchaud*) and night light (*veilleuse*), the topmost section with its candle-socket finial serving as a cover for the two-handled bowl beneath. The contents of the bowl would be warmed by a candle set in the small dish at the base.

13. **Vase.** Soft paste. H. 6$\frac{5}{16}$ in. (16 cm.)
Mark: fleur-de-lis in underglaze blue
Naples, Capodimonte, ca. 1750
Gift of R. Thornton Wilson, 1950, in memory of Florence Ellsworth Wilson
50.211.266
Pulcinella was one of three commedia-dell'arte characters of Neapolitan origin and the only one to be habitually represented in multiple form. As suggested by the design of the rim, this piece may originally have had a cover, though there are no signs of wear.

14. **Pair of vases.** Soft paste. H. 7½ in. (19.1 cm.), 7⅜ in. (18.7 cm.)
Mark: fleur-de-lis in underglaze blue on each
Naples, Capodimonte, ca. 1755–59
Gift of R. Thornton Wilson, 1950, in memory of Florence Ellsworth Wilson
50.211.267,268

15. **Saucer and beaker with decoration in relief on pink ground.** Soft paste. Diam. of saucer 6$\frac{1}{16}$ in. (15.4 cm.), H. of beaker 2¾ in. (7 cm.)
Mark: fleur-de-lis in underglaze blue on saucer
Naples, Capodimonte, ca. 1743
The Charles E. Sampson Memorial Fund, 1983
1983.95.1,2

16. **Snuffbox with gold rims.** Soft paste. W. 3½ in. (8.9 cm.)
Model by Giuseppe Gricci
Box rim inscribed: *Franc^us Pignataro Panormi^us F. Neapoli*
Naples, Capodimonte, ca. 1745
Gift of R. Thornton Wilson, 1955, in memory of Florence Ellsworth Wilson
55.216.4
The model is first mentioned in 1743. The miniature inside the lid is possibly by the factory painter Giovanni Caselli; the gold mounts are the only known work of the Palermo goldsmith Francesco Pignataro.

17. **Mater Dolorosa.** Soft paste. H. 15½ in. (39.4 cm.)
Signed: G *GRICC* incised under glaze
Model by Giuseppe Gricci
Naples, Capodimonte, ca. 1744
Gift of Douglas Dillon, 1971
1971.92.1
Acquired with a slightly larger unsigned figure of St. John the Evangelist, perhaps by a different modeler. This is the only known signed work by Gricci and may be the *figura della Pietà* referred to in the factory records as having been modeled by him in 1744.

18. **Dancing Couple.** Soft paste. H. 8¼ in. (21 cm.)
Naples, Capodimonte, 1750–55
Gift of Douglas Dillon, 1982
1982.450.1

19. **Pottery Vendor.** Soft paste. H. 8⅛ in. (20.6 cm.)
Model attributed to Giuseppe Gricci
Mark: fleur-de-lis in underglaze blue
Naples, Capodimonte, ca. 1745
Gift of Douglas Dillon, 1982
1982.450.4
One of a series of figures of street vendors and peddlers referred to in 1744 and 1745 as *figure che rappresentano poveri.*

20. **Pulcinella.** Soft paste. H. 10 in. (25.4 cm.)
Naples, Capodimonte, 1745–50
Gift of R. Thornton Wilson, 1950, in memory of Florence Ellsworth Wilson
50.211.264
In his right hand Pulcinella holds spaghetti, the strands of which are now missing. A wedge of cheese and a grater are on the ground beside him.

21. **The Rabbit Catchers.** Soft paste. H. 6 7/16 in. (16.4 cm.)
Naples, Capodimonte, 1755–59
The Jack and Belle Linsky Collection, 1982
1982.60.286
The young man is catching hold of a rabbit that has been chased from its hole by a ferret, whose hindquarters and tail are seen in the foreground.

22. **Old Man Dressing.** Soft paste. H. 8⅜ in. (21.3 cm.)
Naples, Capodimonte, ca. 1750
Gift of Douglas Dillon, 1983
1983.488.4
Not certainly identified, the composition may depict a scene from a commedia-dell'arte play.

SELECTED BIBLIOGRAPHY

Charles, Rollo. *Continental Porcelain of the Eighteenth Century,* London, 1964.

Detroit Institute of Arts. *The Golden Age of Naples: Art and Civilization under the Bourbons 1734–1805,* 1981, vol. II.

Detroit Institute of Arts. *The Twilight of the Medici: Late Baroque Art in Florence, 1670–1743,* 1974.

Ginori Lisci, Leonardo. *La porcellana di Doccia,* Milan, 1963.

Lane, Arthur. *Italian Porcelain,* London, 1954.

Molajoli, Bruno, and Giuseppe Liverani. *Il museo delle porcellane di Doccia,* 1967.

Mottola Molfino, Alessandra. *L'arte della porcellana in Italia,* 2 vols., 1976.

Stazzi, Francesco. *L'arte della ceramica Capodimonte,* Milan, 1972.

Porcellane della casa eccellentissima Vezzi, Milan, 1967.

Le porcellane veneziane di Geminiano e Vincenzo Cozzi, Venice, n.d.

ISBN 9780300200805

9 780300 200805